BULLETPROOF YOUR BUSINESS

How To Survive And Thrive In Any Economy

Rick Cottrell

INDIE BOOKS
INTERNATIONAL®

ISBN-13: 978-1-952233-55-5
Library of Congress Control Number: 2021905210

Designed by Joni McPherson, mcphersongraphics.com

INDIE BOOKS INTERNATIONAL, INC®
2424 VISTA WAY, SUITE 316
OCEANSIDE, CA 92054

www.indiebooksintl.com

This book is dedicated to entrepreneurs who are tired of the status quo, want more from their business and lives, and are willing to do something about it, including "burning their boats," and never looking back.

CONTENTS

PART I

Why Strive For The Best And Prepare For The Worst?

Can completing a process to scale growth really result in the next-level success you desire?

I'm here to tell you it can—and here's a true story that proves it (name and some details changed to protect confidentiality).

> *Meet John Smith, CEO and owner of a $10 million commercial contracting business.*
>
> *Every day was Groundhog Day[1] to John. He usually arrived in the office at 5 a.m. at least six days a week and had a sixty-plus-hour work week, always with the best of intentions, trying to keep the business going.*
>
> *There was trouble on the home front with his wife and son. John had very little time for them, and hadn't taken a meaningful vacation in more than three years. He was also constantly being dragged into the weeds by his employees, delivering constant frustration and stress.*

When John contacted us, he was at his wit's end, actually asking me how to walk away from his business with minimal liabilities.

I told him he was crazy—that with the size of his industry's potential and the uniqueness of his company, he should be hitting it out of park—he just needed a roadmap to help him get there.

John's story of feeling trapped by his business is a common one. He took over the business from his father seven years before, when it had been growing at about 6 percent per year. Not great, but at least it was growing with the economy.

"Four years ago it hit the ceiling," said John. "The business was recording zero annual growth and not getting any traction, in a time when generating a nice profit was almost a given."

John knew there was a better way—but he didn't know how to get there.

Here was the problem: John was conditioned to the status quo; he got used to it. His way of life was built based on the expectation of mediocrity, from his business and himself. It became a bad habit.

This pain wasn't sufficient to drive him to change, though. He had forgotten how to be an entrepreneur. John was basically a W-2 employee for his own company. And frankly, he was not a good leader.

I have found that entrepreneurs, including myself, can be so focused into the depths of their businesses that they forget to consider themselves. They become what I call "entrepreneurial martyrs," foregoing consideration of their own well-being to make sure everyone else and the company is taken care of.

The straightforward process we taught John showed him how to break through the ceiling and achieve next-level success.

His company still has a long way to go, but listen to John now, as he talks of how, not if.

"We've seen our growth exceed 20 percent per year for the last two years," John said. "This year we installed a profit-sharing plan. The future looks bright for us. I'm working thirty to thirty-five hours per week, so I'm able to go to my son's soccer games and my wife likes me again."

What is your future going to look like? Are you going to keep spinning your wheels or turn your back on mediocrity to achieve the success you've always dreamed about?

Time to Bulletproof Your Business

Have you bulletproofed your business?

As I write this, countless small and midsized business owners are learning a very painful lesson about what happens when their company is not protected in the worst of times.

The global upheaval resulting from the coronavirus outbreak is certainly driving home the absolute requirement for businesses to make themselves bulletproof—to be less susceptible to changing socioeconomic and environmental conditions, whether abrupt or gradual.

We won't know the number of business fatalities resulting from the 2020 pandemic until long after it's over, but the past provides sobering data and insights. According to the Federal Emergency Management Agency (FEMA), 40 percent of businesses do not reopen following a disaster, and another 25 percent fail within one year.[2] Additionally, the US Small Business Administration found that over 90 percent of companies fail within two years of being struck by a disaster.[3] You read that right—90 percent, nine of out of ten.

Sadly, according to our research, over 80 percent of small-to-midsized businesses are not prepared to achieve next-level success, let alone withstand adversity. And statistics from past downturns show most are totally unprepared for adversity. For instance, the effect the Great Recession of 2008 had on businesses with less than $5 million in revenue was devastating. Bankruptcies rose 74 percent in

2009, with more than 1 million cases filed in federal courts that year.[4]

"You hear about how many fourth-quarter comebacks that a guy has, and I think it means a guy screwed up in the first three quarters."
Peyton Manning, NFL quarterback

Before I go too much further, let me stop to focus on business owners. Now, you picked up this book and have started to read it, and that's great. However, what kind of an owner are you? Are you satisfied with treading water and being mediocre, or are you tired of the status quo and seeking to get to that next level? And if you're in the latter group, do you have the guts to change?

For every ten business owners I sit down with, on average three will be happy with mediocre results; the other seven want more for themselves and their businesses—they just may not know it. If you're ready to achieve more—and willing to put in the work to grow a scalable business that is bulletproof—this book is for you. If not, we really have nothing to talk about.

Are you satisfied with treading water and being mediocre, or are you tired of the status quo and seeking to get to that next level?

Is that a little harsh for you? I find that many owners of small and midsized businesses lack the toughness necessary to make the best decisions for their organizations. It's why so many mediocre employees are on payrolls—owners are afraid to do what's right for their businesses and get rid of them.

Some people call me a lightning rod; I have developed a reputation as someone who will shake things up for the better. I'm a straight shooter. Nothing candy-coated about me. Nothing I do is personal—it's about helping business owners be successful. Still with me?

CHAPTER 1

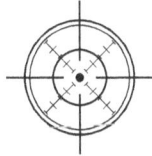

Why You Must Maximize Your Business's Potential Now

"Are you part of the problem, part of the solution, part of the problem with the solution or part of the solution to the problem with the solution?"

GLASBERGEN

When I talk with existing and potential clients, no matter where they are in the world, the level of emotional and irrational state of mind is the greatest when a business has not completely implemented an architecture that prepares it for steady, consistent, and scalable growth.

Most business owners do not yet have the confidence and clarity that comes with having a *fortress of conviction* that their business will survive and thrive, regardless of the threat. Many of them were reeling in light of the unprecedented shutdowns caused by the global pandemic.

I like to analogize the entrepreneurial journey with riding a bike. The pedals power you to where you are going (your business) and the handlebars steer you in the direction you want to go (your why).

Without direction, your business will never achieve its maximum potential. You will always be operating in the unknown.

Unfortunately, far too many business owners are missing both pieces—they don't know where they want to go, and thus they are unaware of what they should be doing right now to fuel success for today and the future. And forget about planning for adversity; that is simply not done in most small-to-midsized businesses.

"Rule Number 1: Never lose money. Rule Number 2: Never forget rule Number 1."
Warren Buffett, American business magnate

Starting Your Journey

To understand how to take your business to the next level, you must start with "you." What do *you* want to get out of your business? I meet with business owners every day who are not satisfied with the performance of their business and discount or exclude themselves from the equation. When I ask the question, "What are you hoping to get out of your business?" they look at me like I am speaking in tongues or say, "Interesting. No one has ever asked me that."

Really?

An understanding of your personal vision is extremely important when taking your business to the next level. We'll talk a lot more about that when we discuss your personal roadmap and how that translates to your business objectives.

You also must discover where your business stands today—whether it's properly prepared for next-level success—and that involves looking at a number of factors, including holistic business health and economic business health. Included in the holistic assessment is a deep dive into six major components common in all businesses. The Entrepreneurial Operating System, or EOS, does a great job of breaking it down, and they include: vision, people, data, issues, process, and traction— or the ability of the entire organization to row in the same direction. The objective is to get these components operating at a minimum of 80 percent strong or better. By doing so, any business can and will achieve next level success.

> *"No matter how brilliant your mind or strategy, if you're playing a solo game, you'll always lose out to a team."*
> **Reid Hoffman, co-founder of LinkedIn**

In addition, the economic and financial side of the business must be evaluated and benchmarked against specific industry standards. And finally, leadership and management must be assessed and compared to best practice benchmarks to determine if the group's makeup can lead the company to next-level success.

MAXIMIZATION OF POTENTIAL

Bill and his partner, Mary, owners of Acme, Inc., a $1.5 million IT services company, knew there was more their business could achieve. They talked about it all the time. They wondered why and how their competitors were doing so well. It seemed like they had the best of intentions to sit down and figure out how to help their hopes, dreams, and wishes materialize through their business— but those meetings never took place; nothing ever happened. Like hundreds of thousands of other small-to-midsized companies, Bill and Mary took their place in the land of status quo, feeling comfortable doing the same old stuff.

Then Bill attended a business lunch that we hosted at his bank on the topic, "How to Maximize the Potential of a Business." He figured the worst that could happen was getting a free lunch and facetime with the bank VP, which could help him when it came time to get his lines of credit renewed.

What Bill found was something he could sink his teeth into—a process he and Mary could use to guide their company to next-level success centered around a scalable growth architecture. It gave them confidence to understand where they were, where they want to go, and a dynamic roadmap to get them there.

Fast forward to sixteen months later: Acme, Inc. surpassed $5 million in top-line sales, the bottom line reflects a double-digit increase, and Bill and Mary have a leadership team that allows them to have an enviable work/life balance.

Acme, Inc. has a long way to go, but unlike most companies its size, it now *gets it* and is set up for future success.

Lessons Learned From COVID-19

Let's go back to COVID-19 for a moment. Some companies were prepared for its impact because they understood a threat was on the horizon. They were talking about the possible effects of a pandemic as early as December 2019, so they had their plans in place before the "shit hit the fan," as they say; they were in a much better position to ride things out than their counterparts, who were blindsided. From a worst-case perspective, being prepared absolutely lessened the short- and long-term impact of the pandemic for these businesses both financial and non-financial because they were structured to do business as usual in what must be called the "new normal."

Let's look at two situations I saw that support the need to maximize your business's potential now as a way to withstand any adversity that comes your way.

The first, a manufacturing company that had its act together with a strong architecture in place for about one year, was already planning on restructuring the business before the COVID-19 restrictions hit. That restructuring included maximizing its current potential and setting itself up for the surge in business projected after the new normal was defined. Basically, in a calm and collected way, this company created its own economy. It never missed a beat.

Contrast that with the e-commerce company that did not have a strong architecture in place, and thus went into panic mode. Management ripped the organization to shreds, driven by fear, basically crossing their fingers, hoping the company could "rise from the ashes" down the line.

If only that company had the time to plan—to withstand the COVID-19 adversity and maybe even thrive—rather than be knocked off course and possibly out of business. Things could have been different if it had just had a mechanism in place to determine what was coming and prepare for it, i.e., the forethought to consider opportunities that might present themselves post-pandemic, regardless of any government assistance offered.

"There cannot be a crisis next week. My schedule is already full."
Henry Kissinger, American diplomat

Like the manufacturing company noted above, many of the businesses that stayed afloat and even thrived during the economic slowdown caused by COVID-19 did their homework before the crisis hit because they had a strong architecture in place:

- Their leadership teams were aligned— something that removed stress from the owner and allowed for more forward-thinking activities, including planning for potential adversity.

- Their business had a strong foundation and operating system everyone bought into.

- They had the right people and resources, giving them the ability to rearrange personnel if that became necessary, rather than shed people as a first step.

- They had a dynamic roadmap created by using hard data, which allowed them to focus on achieving scalable growth while also preparing for a worst-case scenario.

Those four elements are at the heart of the Scalable Growth Architecture (SGA)—they are the four building blocks of a prepared and scalable business. We will get much deeper into them in the next chapter. At this juncture, as we focus on why maximizing your business's potential now is necessary, suffice to say that having all four building blocks in place—prioritized leadership, a strong operating foundation, the right people and resources, and a dynamic roadmap—is crucial for any business that seeks consistent, scalable growth and a path to overcoming any adversity that comes its way.

"The politicians say 'we' can't afford a tax cut. Maybe we can't afford the politicians."
Steve Forbes, editor-in-chief of Forbes Media

The Opportunities Are There

Some owners are just lazy, content with the status quo, and blind to the potential for scalable growth. Others are egomaniacs who think they know everything, yet they lack the focus and know-how to capitalize on the opportunities that are right in front of them.

"Success is going from failure to failure without loss of enthusiasm."
Winston Churchill, prime minister of the United Kingdom

I sincerely hope you are neither of those types of business owners, and you are truly intent on investing in developing a scalable business. If you genuinely want to maximize your business's potential because you understand that by doing so, you put yourself in a better position to ride out the downturns and maximize growth, you're part of the reason I wrote this book.

Frankly, which business owner would you want to be in the following scenario?

> **Owner A** did not prepare his business for adversity and is facing bankruptcy.

> **Owner B** did prepare his business for lean times—and he's looking forward to the

chance of buying Owner A's company at "fire sale" prices.

We will soon get into the meat of the book: how to take your business to the next level. But first, I want you to feel confident in my ability to steer you in the right direction, so let me take down the curtain, so to speak, and share my story with you—warts and all. While I spend my time today working with business owners on their businesses, I have been in your shoes. Both my successes and my failures made me the person I am today, someone with the experience, firsthand knowledge, and tools to help support your dreams of maximizing your business's potential right now.

BULLET DODGERS

Why You Must Maximize Your Business's Potential Now

1. When you prepare your business for scalability and growth, in essence, you are also preparing it to deal with any unforeseen curveballs.

2. Having in place four building blocks— prioritized leadership, a strong operating foundation, the right people and resources, and a dynamic roadmap—is crucial for any business that seeks consistent, scalable growth and a path to overcoming any adversity that comes its way.

CHAPTER 2

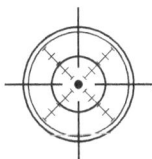

How To Bulletproof Your Business: My Mess To Success

"How come you never bring me any of your stupid ideas anymore?"

GLASBERGEN
©Glasbergen

I consider myself to be unemployable, and if you're an entrepreneurial business owner, you know what I mean. Those of us with entrepreneurial minds probably can't answer *yes* to the question, "Could I work for someone else?" But like many people, I came to that conclusion after getting my feet wet by working in corporate America.

> **The benefit of having firsthand experience—of going through the ups and downs associated with business ownership—simply cannot be duplicated.**

Although I was raised with old-world thinking—you go to school, get a job, work for years, and retire—I think my brain was wired to question that traditional way to live life. During my school years, I was constantly asking *why*, since academia and logic didn't seem to mix for me. But I still earned a bachelor's degree in medical technology and a master's degree in technology management (IT). It provided some value, but not how to proceed as an entrepreneur.

I also had a strong role model in my mother. My father died when I was sixteen. My mom and I had a comfortable middle-class life, but I witnessed her decision to leave her job, buy a business, and successfully run and grow it for many years. If she didn't feel like going into work one day, she didn't have to—because she had hired good people to handle day-to-day operations—and she had built a lifestyle others would envy.

"Luck is a dividend of sweat. The more you sweat, the luckier you get."
Ray Kroc, founder of McDonald's Corporation

Once my schooling was behind me, I was lucky enough to get a job at EDS, Ross Perot's company. I say lucky because EDS was small at that time and had an entrepreneurial culture; employees were routinely encouraged to think through and solve problems rather than relying on others for solutions.

After EDS was acquired by General Motors, I was selected to go to Detroit and participate in the integration of the EDS "way" into the Chevrolet Motor Division. The entrepreneurial environment—making significant decisions and having no prescribed structure—appealed to me, but ultimately, my tasks became routine and I was bored.

My next assignment was more to my liking: leading a team that designed, developed, and implemented customer engagement and assistance centers around the world, which included building the facilities, hiring people, implementing technology, and working with budgets in the $50+ million range. At the conclusion of that project, a consulting firm from Washington, DC I had worked with offered me an autonomous position where I could flex my independence and further develop my entrepreneurial mind.

"For a list of all the ways technology has failed to improve the quality of life, please press three."
Alice Kahn, American writer

This opportunity appealed to me for professional and personal reasons. It allowed me to be more than just an employee, and I was from DC, so I would be moving home, so to speak—and my mom would have her only child close to her. This position was a dream come true. I was able to travel globally and implement solutions that helped companies increase their sales and grow. It was a who's-who of quality organizations including Apple, Marriott, BMW, Avis, and Kraft Foods.

After about three years, I realized some things about myself: I got bored as soon as a job became routine and I needed something that would deliver a better personal ROI to keep me motivated. I decided it was time for me to go out on my own.

Other People's Money

In my early thirties, I saw an opportunity, used the knowledge I had gained, put together a business plan to create a database marketing company that would serve the car industry, and got some investors to bite. Those years were heady; I was working with a partner, someone who was my mentor, and I didn't turn down any opportunity. I was a "hand raiser," and on one occasion I was asked by General Motors purchasing if we could do all the NASCAR motor sports marketing on behalf of the UAW. Heck yeah! A couple million in new business, "We got that."

"If at first you don't succeed, try, try again. Then quit. There's no point in being a damn fool about it."

W.C. Fields, American comedian and actor

That hand-raiser mentality paid dividends for us. We were up for anything that even bordered on our core competency. We didn't, however, have complete autonomy, since we were using money from investors. Ultimately, we sold the company— and I decided to take the plunge and buy a company myself.

Wholesaling & Distributing Success

All told, I've had fourteen companies—which includes acquiring some to support my existing companies in areas like advertising, digital marketing, and internet bandwidth. But the first company I purchased without the benefit of investor support was a wholesale distributor specializing in home furnishings and remodeling products based in St. Louis that had about 750 customers and a handful of employees.

The location would get my wife closer to her family, and you know what they say: happy wife, happy life. And she was an integral part of the operation, serving as the COO for eighteen years until we sold the company in 2018.

Before I made the acquisition, I did my homework, researching the future of the industry and the company's "bones" to determine if the opportunity for growth was there. I believed then and still believe today that as long as you have a scalable mindset, you can look at a business as something that can be grown and taken to the next level. It should not be a question of *if* you see potential, but *how* you can access that potential by properly structuring the company.

"Why join the Navy if you can be a pirate?"
Steve Jobs, American business magnate

I knew inherently that the platform for success was to follow what makes franchises work so well: consistency and predictability. And while I hadn't yet coined the Scalable Growth Architecture (SGA), I followed what would become its tenets religiously—prioritizing leadership, developing a strong operating foundation, securing the right people and resources, and creating a dynamic roadmap. In particular, I constantly worked to enhance my leadership skills because I knew success always starts at the top.

While I was the picture of bravado outwardly, the fact that every dollar I spent was mine—not investment money—was never far from my mind. I didn't have a safety net, but I was confident in the concept of beating the prices customers were paying elsewhere while still retaining my margins. And I didn't have to eat the whole apple, so to speak; I never considered industry giants like Home Depot and Lowe's to be my competition.

I also knew to grow—regardless of what your business does or makes—you must become a sales and marketing machine that just happens to do what it is you do. From 2002 to 2018, my TV advertising budget alone was about $1 million a year; we were out there, while our average competition's sales and marketing efforts were primitive and held back by fear.

"If you see a bandwagon, it's too late."
James Goldsmith, British-French financier

I don't proclaim to be a genius, but I did a lot of things right over the thirty-five years I ran the businesses I had my hands in and on. I understood the value of having connectivity to subject matter experts—I didn't need to hire someone to gain expertise. I knew how important it was to initiate and maintain relationships with resources in the worlds of banking, accounting, and law. I realized how critical it was to build a dream team and have a solid operating platform. I had a ten-year plan that was driven by my personal objectives, and I was totally committed to making it work.

Of course, there were some stumbles. Because my business was driven by consumer engagement metrics, I spent a lot of time working both *at* it and *on* it—missing out on precious time with my family. It might be considered trite to say kids grow up fast and you can never get back the moments you weren't there for, but it's true. I also made plenty of poor spending decisions, neglected to conduct appropriate due diligence, and spectacularly failed to sufficiently vet quite a few business opportunities. There were a lot of lessons learned.

Those who don't know why they're doing something are doomed to inherent inefficiency.

Fortunately, my good decisions far outweighed my bad. The company endured the economic uncertainty that occurred in the recession of the early 2000s, 9/11, and the 2008 housing industry fiasco. We prepared for adversity by looking ahead, discussing issues that could affect the business. We approached suppliers to gauge their needs so we could be on top of what they wanted. We moved online and bought two showrooms in the St. Louis area as well. We maxed out at sixty employees, more than 8,000 customers, and top-line sales in the area of $25 million with a net return on sales that would be the envy of companies twice the size.

"Being powerful is like being a lady. If you have to tell people you are, you aren't."
Margaret Thatcher, prime minister of the United Kingdom

To me, there was no mystery as to why I was successful. Everything I did was driven by the use of consistent processes and practices. Plus, I knew my personal *why* was aligned with my business *why*. Those who don't know why they're doing something are doomed to inherent inefficiency. And those who are satisfied with mediocrity are doomed to remain there, at a comfort level that perhaps doesn't maximize the potential of their company. I was never one of those people. Are you?

BULLET DODGERS

How To Bulletproof Your Business: My Mess to Success

1. As long as you have a scalable mindset, you can look at a business as something that can be grown and taken to the next level.

2. It should not be a question of if you see potential, but how you can access that potential by properly structuring the company.

3. Realize that no matter what you do, you're merely a sales- and marketing-driven company that just happens to make or do something.

4. If you don't know why you're doing something, you're doomed to inherent inefficiency.

PART II

How To Take Your Business To The Next Level

If you read the first section rather than skipping the *why* to get to the *how to*, my hope is that you're now chomping at the bit to learn what you must do to take your business to the next level. If you skipped the first section, you missed out on some valuable information that could very well be the difference between building a scalable business or falling short.

Hey, I know you're busy; that's why I purposely made this entire book a short read. I know I don't have time to read or listen to lengthy books, and I figure you don't, either.

So now we get to the meat of the matter. You understand why it's important to bulletproof your business, take advantage of opportunities today, and protect it from future adversity. You aren't satisfied with mediocrity/the status quo; you want a predictably scalable business, but don't know how to take it to the next level.

This section focuses on the two most critical tasks you must complete on your journey to long-term business success: determining your personal roadmap and defining your SGA. Ready to dive in?

CHAPTER 3

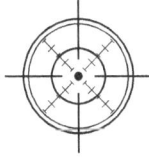

Determine Your Personal Roadmap

©Glasbergen / glasbergen.com

"I can claim a 70-inch plasma TV as a business
expense because my accountant said it's
important to look at the big picture."

41

In their quest to run successful businesses, many owners of small and midsized companies neglect to consider their own objectives and goals. They get so bogged down in the minutiae of daily operations that their personal needs fall by the wayside, and with no focus on why they're doing what they do, they are, in essence, steering a rudderless ship.

Most business owners have to work hard for success; being lucky, or in the right place at the right time (like facemask manufacturers in the time of COVID-19) is a one in a million occurrence.

Regardless of what goals you have for your business, you can never forget that the personal return you receive—such as the ability to send your kids to college, pay for your dad's assisted living facility, and enjoy the lifestyle you desire—must be a driving force for you. Most business owners have to work hard for success; being lucky, or in the right place at the right time (like facemask manufacturers in the time of COVID-19) is a one-in-a-million occurrence. And it's even harder to be successful when you really don't know why you're working so hard.

To assist you with that *why*, we've created the following Roadmap for the Bulletproof Entrepreneur.

Roadmap for the Bulletproof Entrepreneur

1 | **PERSONAL "WHY"—OBJECTIVES AND GOALS**
WHAT DO YOU WANT OUT OF LIFE?

2 | **PERSONAL ECONOMICS & LIFE BALANCE**
WHAT DOES IT LOOK LIKE?

DREAMING TO ACHIEVING

3 | **BUSINESS "WHY"—OBJECTIVES AND GOALS**
HOW WILL YOUR BUSINESS SUPPORT YOUR PERSONAL WHY?

4 | **BUSINESS ECONOMIC & TARGET SCALABILITY**
WHAT DOES IT LOOK LIKE?

It seems straightforward, right? But when I have asked owners of small and midsize businesses to share their personal *why* with me—something that drives the rest of the roadmap—most of them have no idea. That's a problem.

As we dig down into the roadmap, you'll see that having the answers to the questions it poses will provide you with not just greater focus, but with the ability to make decisions that will support both your *why*, and that of your business.

Personal Why—Objectives And Goals: What Do You Want Out Of Life?

Having specific objectives and goals for your life is key to being able to create a scalable business that can withstand adversity. Why? Because without them, you're likely to lose your edge as well as your ability to focus—and I actually lived this.

When our wholesaling business was in its heyday, we had money to do absolutely anything we wanted. But when you can buy everything you ever dreamed of, you start to believe you don't need to have objectives and goals to keep you moving forward. A sort of malaise kicks in that doesn't promote big-picture planning. As the adage says, "Profit hides lots of mistakes."

This is one of the most important things I work on with my clients. For instance, the owner of an e-commerce company was thrilled to see his annual revenue hit $1 million. But when I asked him if he had life insurance, he said no. He immediately saw the need for it when I uncovered that one of his personal *whys* was ensuring he could support all the dreams of his wife and kids.

Personal Economics And Life Balance: What Does That Look Like?

Once you've identified your personal *whys*, you must determine the economics required to support them. This has a lot to do with work/life balance, i.e., how hard you're willing to work to achieve the lifestyle you desire.

Let's estimate that most business owners put in sixty hours a week. If you're willing to do that, great. But if you aren't, if you want to limit your time to forty hours a week so you can be with family more, you have to figure out what resources are needed to bridge that twenty-hour gap.

"By working faithfully eight hours a day you may eventually get to be the boss and work twelve hours a day."
Robert Frost, American poet

Put another way, the personal objectives and goals you set in item number 1 of the roadmap were based on your putting in a specific level of effort. If you want to put in less effort because you want to "live life," you need to determine a strategy to ensure you're still able to achieve those objectives and goals.

This reminds me of a client I actually had to fire. He had some impressive personal objectives and goals, but he only wanted to work part-time and wasn't willing to hire someone (spend money) to manage things when he wasn't around. He wanted all the spoils, but he wasn't willing to put in the hard work to earn them.

Business "Why"—Objectives And Goals: How Will Your Business Support Your Personal Why?

I find the small minority of business owners who have even attempted to consider why they do what they do often start here, with a focus on their business's objectives and goals. It's better than doing nothing, since those comprise the engine that support roadmap items 1 and 2, but most of these owners are miserable.

When you set business objectives and goals— which typically include specific customer numbers or revenue marks to achieve—without having personal objectives and goals as a backstop, you can literally work yourself to death. You probably know owners of small and midsize businesses who never have time for anything outside work; they're always toiling to hit their numbers and missing out on things like seeing their kids grow up, enjoying hobbies, or even just taking it easy once in a while.

It's not possible to have a bulletproof business without being a bulletproof entrepreneur.

If you're stressing yourself out to the point that your quality of life, or even your health, is negatively affected, you're playing a dangerous game. It's possible to reset by going back to items 1 and 2 of the roadmap and setting your personal objectives and goals, focusing on what you want your life to look like. That is the best path toward achieving a scalable business.

Business Economics And Target Scalability: What Does It Look Like?

This is the point where you need to dig in to determine the top-line number or profitability (aka the metrics) your business must produce to support your personal objectives and goals. This includes considering what level of investment is required—in human resources, etc.—to ensure your business can achieve it.

To use an extremely simplistic example, let's say you need $1 a month to support your personal objectives and goals. That means you need to sell

$4 every month or risk being personally unhappy. Put another way, if your business sells enough each month to cover your costs, but there is nothing or very little left for you, is that really the kind of success you're aiming for?

BULLET DODGERS

Determine Your Personal Roadmap

1. If you're so bogged down in the minutiae of daily operations that your personal needs fall by the wayside and you aren't focused on why you're doing what you do, you are, in essence, steering a rudderless ship.

2. The personal return you receive from your business must be a driving force for you.

3. Having specific objectives and goals for your life is key to being able to create a scalable business that can withstand adversity.

4. It's not possible to have a bulletproof business without being a bulletproof entrepreneur.

CHAPTER 4

Define Your Scalable Growth Architecture

©Glasbergen / glasbergen.com

GLASBERGEN

"I'm not lacking leadership skills.
Everyone else is lacking followship skills!"

THE BULLETPROOF BUSINESS®

PRIORITIZED
LEADERSHIP

THE RIGHT PEOPLE
AND RESOURCES

A DYNAMIC
ROADMAP

A STRONG OPERATING FOUNDATION

THE SCALABLE GROWTH ARCHITECTURE® (SGA®)

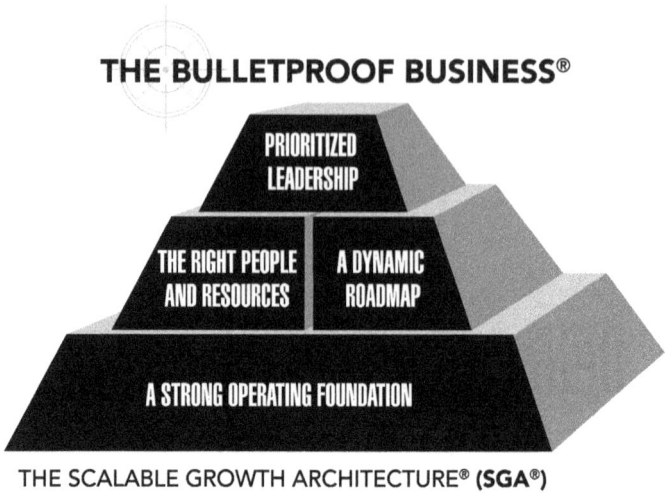

So now we get to the meatiest part of the sandwich, so to speak. You know why you should maximize your business's potential to be predictably scalable and able to withstand adversity, and you have a personal roadmap to ensure you don't lose sight of your own objectives and goals as you work hard to build your business. Now, you need to know what to do to take your business to the next level.

I previously introduced the Scalable Growth Architecture (SGA), but here is where we take a deep dive into it. The illustration above shows the SGA building blocks; to be predictably scalable, a business must have it together in all four.

The journey to building a predictably scalable business requires a discovery process that takes into account subjective and objective evaluation. Gaps are identified, prioritized, and filled. We have found every business has a different set of circumstances affecting each of the four building blocks. But rest assured that the circumstances, as unique as they may appear on the surface, never prevent a business from achieving a bulletproof status and achieving next-level success if the desire to do so is present.

There is no defined order in which the SGA must be addressed—it will vary from business to business, depending on where it stands with regard to each building block at the beginning of the process. Let's take a look at each of them, one by one.

Prioritized Leadership

THE BULLETPROOF BUSINESS®

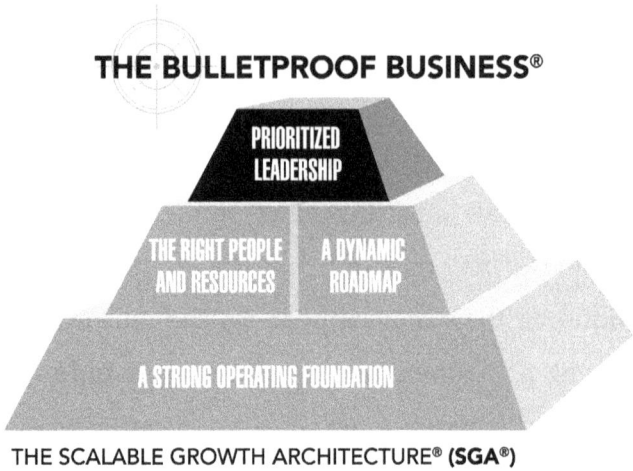

THE SCALABLE GROWTH ARCHITECTURE® (SGA®)

The building block we will start with is prioritized leadership, since success always starts at the top. While you certainly need great people in an organization, history has shown time and time again that a rudderless company will never achieve maximum potential. It will not even come close.

Strong leaders are characterized by their investment in personal and organizational growth and their commitment to keeping the right priorities in the right order.

Companies can only reach their desired levels of health, productivity, and profitability if their leaders model attitudes and behaviors worth following. Strong leaders are characterized by their investment in personal and organizational growth and their commitment to keeping the right priorities in the right order. According to Brandon Schaefer (founder and CEO of Five Capitals) and collaborative partner TTI Success Insights, companies who see the most long-term success hold fast to the Prioritized Leader Framework (see below). Together Schaefer and TTI Success Insights have created an entire product suite, to help organization's maximize cultural health, productivity and profitability. Here is the Prioritized Leader Framework:

- **Priority 1—Purpose**: The vision to see, articulate, and go for a compelling future (Leadership currency is integrity and inspiration.)

- **Priority 2—People**: The level of health and productivity we have with our colleagues and connections (Leadership currency is encouragement and accountability.)

- **Priority 3 — Pace**: Discerning how slowly or quickly the organization and its personnel need to move to sustain long-term success, maximize opportunities, and grow capital (Leadership currency is time and energy.)

- **Priority 4 — Perception**: Choosing a growth mindset and staying open to creative solutions and new ideas (Leadership currency is insight and innovation.)

- **Priority 5 — Profit**: The effective management, investment, and release of an organization's resources (Leadership currency is dollars and cents.)

The perspective most needed to achieve next-level success today is closely tied to the leader. Great leaders must have a vision that is bigger than themselves. They need to have the ability to be both humble and direct. They must encourage and empower those around them, while speaking truth and confronting reality as they see it. This will allow leaders to confront the brutal facts of today, yet keep an unwavering hope in the future.[5]

"Don't be afraid to give up the good to go for the great."

John D. Rockefeller, American oil tycoon and philanthropist

Leaders who live out the right perspective bring inspiration, energy, collaboration, and focus to those around them. Level 5 leaders (a term coined by leadership expert John C. Maxwell) generate more synergy and productivity than individual members could ever produce on their own. They lead with humble confidence as well as courageous action. This is the perspective necessary to go after greatness in business today.

The Role Of Emotional Intelligence

What else separates great leaders from those who are just mediocre? A great leader is always prepared and has developed the emotional intelligence to work through any opportunity or challenge to understand themselves and how they are bound to react in different situations. They also understand the impact and ramifications their behavior has on others.

Consider what occurred after I facilitated a day-long session with five company leaders and the owner. At the end of our eight hours together, I asked the participants to give me one takeaway, rate the meeting, and let me know if their expectations were met. All the leaders had significant takeaways, gave the meeting high marks, and said their expectations were more than met. The owner, whose facial expression looked like she'd just eaten a lemon, destroyed everything we'd done in one fell swoop by noting that her goal was learning how to generate more revenue right now, and she didn't see that happen. Something that was never on the agenda or identified when the expectations were set.

This woman clearly had no idea that her behavior would set the company back—she had no idea how to be a leader. She didn't listen to the process and ignored all the good feelings her leadership team had about the day. Frankly, without a charismatic leader, most businesses will not find success using the SGA and will be doomed to mediocrity or failure.

> *"Never try to teach a pig to sing. It wastes your time and annoys the pig."*
> **George Bernard Shaw, English playwright**

The Role Of Potential

I've met many business owners who have created an artificial ceiling for themselves and won't rise above it. They have what I call status quo thinking; they operate in a vacuum and don't know the potential their business really has.

These types of owners should take a page from the arachnid world. Spiders will build a web anywhere it seems possible. At a meeting on the fifty-ish floor of a building in Manhattan, I noticed a spider was crawling outside of the glass and was going up. My first thought was, "That spider has no ceiling." It just kept going up, it has no concept of ceiling.

From a business perspective, the message is clear: Why stop before you know how high you can go?

Many business owners place artificial barriers to success. I do most of my work with companies that "hit the ceiling." They stop at a number and remain there for years. It's easy to max out if you don't push yourself and your people. You will leave a lot of potential on the table. There is no reason why a $3M company can't be a $10M, $20M or even a $50M company. Some have the capacity to lead this type of growth, and some do not. But in many cases, if you hit a ceiling, the barrier to going higher is often your ability to leave the status quo behind.

One other comment about leadership. It is alarming to see the number of business owners who do not use the dynamics of peer groups to help them succeed. Whether it is the result of ego or ignorance, they are missing the boat. There is true value in working with a peer group of entrepreneurial business owners. Regardless of industry, my companies P&L always included a line item for involvement in some form of mastermind process.[6] There are quite a few out there and I have participated in more than my fair share. Each one had characteristics that provided value to me and my businesses. In fact, I still participate in a mastermind group and maintain the philosophy that if I get one good idea per year it more than pays for itself. In one instance, we achieved tax savings in excess of $100K based on a suggestion from one of my fellow mastermind participants. Enough savings for eight years of mastermind group cost.

Do You Have The Right Leaders?

Even if you're an outstanding leader, as a business owner, you also need to surround yourself with a similarly outstanding leadership team. If you're going to scale a business, you want to have a pretty good understanding as to whether or not your leaders are a fit, something that can be determined using readily available subjective and objective measures.

On the subjective side, it's whether they pass the "eye" test. For example, using tools that are inherent in the EOS business operating system—the People Analyzer and GWC—are they getting it, wanting it, and do they have the capacity to excel in that function? Also important is whether they exhibit the core values of the company 24/7. Simply put, if they don't, they shouldn't make the cut.

Then comes objectivity measures, the analytics gained by using assessment tools like the TTI Success Insights TriMetrix platform. With this tool, you can measure their *why*, the driving forces of the person or why they get out of bed each morning. It also measures their *how*—how they think, how they work, their behaviors in their natural state, and their skills, competencies, and experiences, as well as if they are able to handle adversity and are aware of how others perceive them.

As a business owner, you must determine whether your leadership team can help your organization scale and grow—understanding this through key role definition, benchmark creation, and determining the probability of success. And you're not done yet.

The secondary component, critically important as a company grows, is whether these folks have the capacity to get better. Can they excel personally and professionally? What is their max ceiling? Determining that, in advance, can lead to a recipe that will help your business achieve maximum potential.

You don't want to get into this situation: You're running a company, investing in scaling and growing and assuming one of your leaders is going to fit when you break through the ceiling and become a vested part of the leadership team (i.e., replacing you). Only then you find out they have no interest in or equity in the "ownership mentality."

We see this over and over again. Companies that fall into this trap will never get out of their own way and ultimately will be in a lesser position in terms of value-consistent performance. Of course, it's a great deal for another entrepreneur looking to pick up a business inexpensively.

Without that entrepreneurial comfort, that group of leaders in place who have potential, you're going to be out of luck. Of course, you also need strong people to complement your leadership team, and that brings us to the next SGA building block.

The Right People And Resources

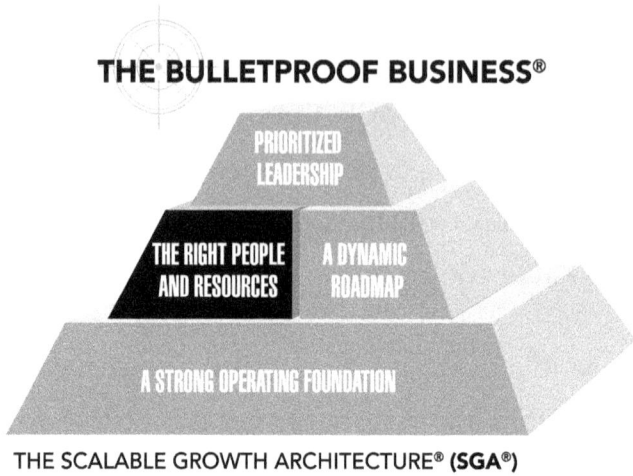

THE BULLETPROOF BUSINESS®

PRIORITIZED
LEADERSHIP

THE RIGHT PEOPLE
AND RESOURCES

A DYNAMIC
ROADMAP

A STRONG OPERATING FOUNDATION

THE SCALABLE GROWTH ARCHITECTURE® **(SGA®)**

Despite all the information out there regarding the need to have the right people in the right seats, businesses continue to hire the wrong people or place the right people in the wrong seats.

The money wasted on poor hiring and onboarding practices is significant. A CareerBuilder survey found companies lost an average of $14,900 on every bad hire,[7] and that does not include lost opportunity dollars. A 2015 Leadership IQ survey found that 46 percent of all new hires are deemed failures by the eighteen-month mark.[8] That's a lot of money lost on hopes, dreams, and wishes.

Most small-to-midsize businesses use something very close to *fog-the-mirror* hiring practices and accept anyone who inhales oxygen. They do not realize that by digging a little deeper, they can determine the true probability of success a person will have in their company.

Since 85 percent of issues businesses have relate to their people (according to EOS Worldwide), you would think businesses would want to get as close as possible to a probability of 100 percent success. And, yes, there are numerous ways to determine whether or not someone fits into your organization and can be a productive part of helping you achieve your business's maximum potential.

Consider these categories:

- **Their Why**—What gets them out of bed in the morning? Why are they coming to work? What motivates them? What drives them? Can they get on board with your vision? Does it sync up with their why?

- **Their How**—What are their behaviors? How do they communicate? Are their behaviors compatible with their role and with their team?

- **Their Competencies/Experiences**—Do their competencies and experiences sync up with their job description, key roles, and accountabilities? If not, can they be coached? Are you prepared to manage someone who has a deficiency in a competency that can't be improved?

- **Their Emotional Intelligence**—This is a big one: If prospective employees have checked all the boxes, how do you know they can handle workspace or personal adversity? You can hire people who have a 100 percent probability of success to do the job, but, if they cannot handle emotional adversity, i.e., problems at home, their productivity will certainly drop, plus they are a "flight risk"—they will walk into your office one day and give you their notice and your jaw will hit the table.

Based on research my firm has conducted, less than 10 percent of businesses truly benchmark their key positions using that criteria, let alone other positions that are instrumental in getting them to next-level success. The expense to find and retain great people is significant—SHRM estimates the cost of recruiting, hiring, and onboarding a new employee can be as much as $240,000[9]—but the cost to benchmark a key position in a business is merely a rounding error. So why don't more companies do it? Experience shows it usually comes down to time and money, with the latter representing the cost to effectively determine fit, not the actual cost of an online job posting.

Consider this example: Let's say a midlevel manager with a fully burdened cost of $75K is hired based on the fiction that is his résumé and his likeability without any analytics (as described above). That means he is onboarded without any knowledge related to his why, how, competencies, and emotional intelligence—so he is being hired with a *roll-the-dice* mentality.

Right out of the gate, a company does not know what to expect out of this individual—starting with how he communicates outside of his interview mask. The damage that can be done culturally because his why is not in sync with the company's vision, for example, can be devastating to an organization that wants to scale and grow. Not to mention that ineffectiveness leads to lower profits, operational inefficiencies, and lost opportunity dollars.

The value of gathering intelligence on prospective and existing employees to ensure you put the right people in the right seats is worth its weight in gold. If you're not routinely doing that, your business cannot scale and succeed. Also consider that research from SHRM[10] shows 69 percent of employed people are passively looking for another job, so perhaps not giving their all to you; my opinion is companies just aren't trying hard enough.

You can actually screw up when it comes to people in three different ways:

Example 1—Wrong person in the company

Example 2—Wrong person in right seat

Example 3—Right person in wrong seat

The question to consider for each of these cases is this: Can you get maximum potential out of your business with that individual in that seat? If not, you are automatically behind the curve.

Here's a story that makes my point. This company was hitting the ceiling. Operational leadership was critical, but cost wasn't managed very well. The function manager exhibited the core values of the company and was a team player—all the things you want out of somebody who would fit in that role— but he could not execute the role effectively because he did not have what it took to make that function happen, driving cultural problems and significant lost opportunity dollars.

The key accountabilities that were defined for the position primarily were intrinsic, meaning they could not be trained into the person. Thus, he was never going to be able to satisfy the job requirements; he would always stay a caterpillar, never becoming a butterfly—and the business would suffer.

It's not uncommon that as a company grows and becomes more complex, it becomes very obvious if somebody is not going to be able to carry it through the ceiling once they hit it. And so, the whole concept of developing people to be able to support and grow an organization is a major problem.

When I speak, I'll typically ask for hands raised if anybody has either picked up or read anything in a book that would help them improve their performance, personally or at work. When they're driving, do they listen to material that can help them improve in their job? Very few hands go up if they're being honest.

Another quick story is about my last business, where most of our fifty-plus employees were hourly folks.

We're not talking about rocket scientists; they were just decent, down-to-earth, hard-working people.

"There are two kinds of people: those who do the work and those who take the credit. Try to be in the first group; there is less competition there."
Indira Gandhi, prime minister of India

We created a training program where we reviewed results from the previous week as a part of our status meetings and set up the coming week. We also would select a business book we could use to help in employee development—a book like *Think and Grow Rich* by Napoleon Hill, for example. We would review a chapter each week; employees would give their feedback, what they learned, and we'd give them an action item to implement that week.

As we grew, we strayed from that habit and just lost touch with it. But we did implement an employee feedback system; we wanted to know what we could do to better help our employees be more effective in their jobs. We expected to see feedback about needing a bigger break room, more Funyuns in the vending machines, etc. What came back was a surprise to us: the number one issue was the lack of personal and professional development. They really missed that weekly training.

Research from SHRM shows our employees were not unique; only one-third of employees (32 percent) are very satisfied with their organization's commitment to professional development.[11] The right people want professional and personal development as part of their engagement with a company.

One final thought about the right people. I cannot stress enough the importance of having a consistent process when onboarding new employees. The statistics are stark and real; according to SHRM, 69 percent of employees are more likely to stay with a company for three years if they experienced great onboarding,[12] and organizations with a standard onboarding process experience 50 percent greater new-hire productivity.[13]

That's right. Poorly onboarded employees will not stay with your organization and their productivity will suffer. Not only that, they will tell everyone they know how crappy a company you run. The amount of resource waste that occurs in the United States resulting from poor onboarding practices could fund a third-world country.

I see it day in and day out—numerous small-to-midsized companies think they have crossed the finish line when a prospective employee says *yes*. Unfortunately, that is when the moment of truth begins. A company must prove itself daily to its people. If you do not have a professional, well thought out, and consistently executed plan, you have lost the right-people war.

"I don't want yes-men around me. I want everyone to tell the truth. Even if it costs them their jobs."
Samuel Goldwyn, American movie mogul

The Role Of The Right Resources

Equally as important as hiring well is understanding the value of using in-house resources or outsourcing to get things done and accelerate productivity and efficiency. Far too many leaders waste time and money doing things they should be delegating. I agree with Dan Sullivan, owner of Strategic Coach, who counsels clients to change their thinking from *how* to get things done to *who* can get things done, whether that entails using internal or external resources, or a combination of the two.[14]

I saw a great example of this when I was working with a $21 million company that was having issues with marketing. Okay, I was being nice—its marketing stank to high heaven. The experienced marketing person leading the effort was seemingly out of the loop on the latest innovations in the field and her "deliverables" were stats like impressions or visits rather than more concrete measures like ROI or leads generated.

"If I had asked people what they wanted,
they would have said faster horses."
Henry Ford, American industrialist

I told the owner he would be better off working
with a cutting-edge marketing company—one
that could be held accountable for producing solid
metrics—than keeping the function in-house. It's a
question of what gives you the most bang for your
buck, and often, it's not adding people to your staff.
Why do you think so many payroll companies
exist? Many businesses have figured out it makes
sense to outsource that function.

As a business owner, you may also need resources
like investors, legal counsel, insurance professionals,
wealth advisors, and other subject matter experts
to be able to successfully run your organization. A
typical question I hear at peer advisory mastermind
meetings is whether anyone knows a good resource
for X, like a business attorney—and it's often asked
because an issue is afoot. That's really too late to be

making inquiries; that relationship should already be developed.

Having a relationship with a banker is also important, and it surprises me to learn that many business owners have their accounts at the same bank as their personal accounts. They'd be much better off using a commercial bank for their business accounts.

The bottom line: A scalable growth architecture cannot develop a business's maximum potential without using the right resources to achieve next-level success—and many of those resources will be found outside your company.

So, we've discussed the two *people SGA building blocks*. But those people—you, your leadership team, and your employees—need more than just the ability and desire to succeed. Let's start with the role of having a dynamic roadmap.

A Dynamic Roadmap

THE BULLETPROOF BUSINESS®

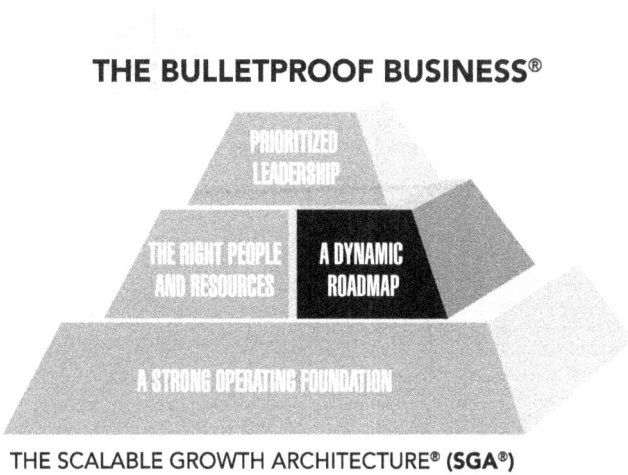

THE SCALABLE GROWTH ARCHITECTURE® **(SGA®)**

Since we live in a world where data is everywhere and easily accessible, it is becoming simpler to develop a dynamic roadmap for next-level success. Owners must have the ability to clearly define where they want their business to go and then create a path or roadmap to track and predict their results, tweaking along the way to enhance the probability of success right around the corner.

Good, hard, reliable data is necessary to develop a dynamic roadmap. Information is required on an ongoing basis since you cannot run a great business without data to help make the right decisions and plan effectively. Today, not only is data necessary, but so is knowing how to use it.

The use of data as a guide to determine how a business got to where it is and where it's going is extremely underdeveloped in small-to-midsized companies.

In fact, our research shows that eight out of ten companies do not have a handle on their data, both noneconomic and economic. This is typically due to the amount of time entrepreneurial business owners spend in their business putting out fires versus working on their businesses. The importance of implementing a platform or operating system to stabilize their business cannot be overstated, as it will give them more freedom to work on their hopeful objective of scalable growth. But that stability must be grounded in the knowledge that a company is running on good information.

All business owners would love to snap their fingers and have access to actionable data that even minimally would tell them how their company is doing. Well, guess what? Most don't.

Why? There are several common challenges to developing actionable business intelligence in the world of small-to-medium-size business, starting with these:

- **The Black Hole Of External Data**—The world we live in now has more useful data than you can possibly imagine. The problem for owners of small-to-medium-sized businesses is determining what is useful for their company and where to find it. Even if owners have time on their hands—which they usually do not—they certainly don't have enough time to embark on a crusade of data discovery.

- **The Lack Of Access To Internal Data**—This is a major roadblock in numerous businesses. On average, when we ask a company for something as simple as a complete set of YTD financials, we see a look of panic in their eyes and hear something to the effect of, "Uhhhh, okay, we'll get right on that." That's just the historical financials; don't get me going on the other key pieces of information required to create scalability in a business that are usually nonexistent.

- **The Uncertain Quality Of Any Data**—This is especially true for internal data. You've probably heard the phrase, *garbage in—garbage out*; it's a real problem when it comes to determining the value of data collected by unverified or unscientific methods.

- **The Lack Of People With Appropriate Skill Sets**—For most small-to-medium-sized businesses, the resources (people) who are in-house are not wired to think about how business intelligence can move a company forward. They are typically in a heads-down position, working tirelessly to do their jobs. Asking them to split business intelligence atoms may not be a key accountability in their role nor will it be part of their competencies. Of course, there are some industries that may be more advanced than others where this is concerned, i.e., a marketing company may have a better handle on key metrics and predicting success than a manufacturing company.

- **The Failure To Prioritize The Importance Of Actionable Business Intelligence**—If the owner does not prioritize the use of data to help the business scale and grow, there is limited hope that it will ever break through the ceiling and achieve next-level success. Of course, there are the lucky few who may get there anyway, but for most of us, it takes hard work and focus. Business owners who do not prioritize the use of data and business intelligence in their organizations are literally missing out on significant cash flow and the opportunity to take their business to the next level.

Developing an actionable business intelligence platform in a small-to-medium-sized business is a journey, a tough journey. But it's definitely worthwhile to put in the work to get to a better place—a place where success becomes an expectation, not just a pipe dream. And, it's important to note that this journey is available to any business in any industry; we have not yet found a business or industry where the following data-development process doesn't hold water and accelerate business scalability and growth:

Step 1—Create a company data warehouse

Step 2—Allocate organizational account-ability to analyze/track and report the data

Step 3—Find the gaps that will deliver the best return on investment and solve them

Step 4—Track the numbers through an effective scorecard and dashboard

Step 5—Develop effective forecasting and the ability to predict business outcomes

Step 6—Inspect the results and improve the company's position—constantly

Taking this journey is akin to participating in an evolutionary process, a walk-before-you-run approach. Unfortunately, you can't jump steps; believe me, I tried and wasted tens of thousands of dollars.

A Strong Operating Foundation

THE BULLETPROOF BUSINESS®

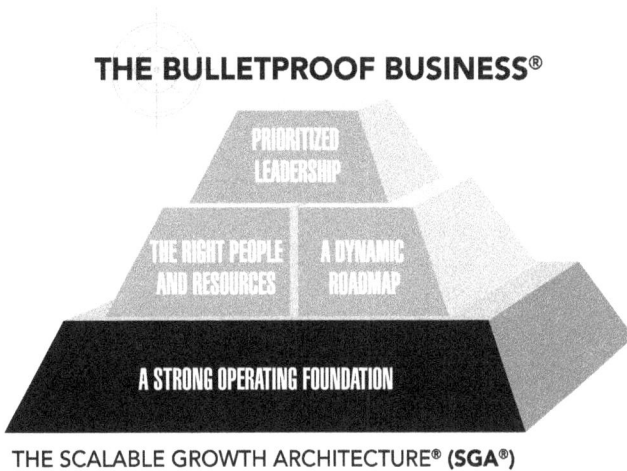

PRIORITIZED LEADERSHIP

THE RIGHT PEOPLE AND RESOURCES

A DYNAMIC ROADMAP

A STRONG OPERATING FOUNDATION

THE SCALABLE GROWTH ARCHITECTURE® (SGA®)

Every business needs a strong operating foundation to protect itself as well as maximize consistency, scalability, and growth. A strong operating foundation brings together all its moving parts, synchronizing its components to achieve its ultimate vision and direction. This is not a technical platform, but a holistic platform that helps get everything in an organization aligned, running efficiently and effectively, and maximizing the potential of the business.

One example of a business operating system is the Entrepreneurial Operating System (EOS). EOS was designed and developed by Gino Wickman and is illustrated and explained in the book *Traction*.[15] As I write this, there are over 10,000 companies using EOS and that number grows every day. The reason why EOS is an attractive solution is its simplicity and ability to generate results very quickly.

The goal of any business operating system is to get everyone in an organization rowing in the same direction. To do that also requires synchronizing all of the moving parts of a business creating a cohesive, finely tuned machine that embodies predictable scalability and growth. Our research shows that 80 percent of small to mid-sized companies operate without a foundational operating system or safety net making them susceptible to any and all adversity, whether big or small.

Entrepreneurially, it is tempting to always be looking at the latest "great idea" by "pick a name" regarding how to run a better business. Unfortunately, far too many business owners and leaders make knee jerk decisions that negatively impact the growth of their company and confuse their people. The one thing that I can say after going through the flavor of the day management approach is—it does not work. Not until I picked a foundational operating system and stuck with it did I find relief.

Therefore, having one business operating system in a company is paramount to its success and longevity. Relying on luck to get from here to there is risky and makes the organization vulnerable to the whims of numerous threats.

Like the operating system that drives the functionality of your smartphone, a business's operating system is the foundation for everything that drives it. However, most companies do not have one. The amount of potential being wasted today from a scalability perspective is truly infinite. Also, the number of business failures due to an unorganized and nonformalized infrastructure is significant. A study done by Staples found 75 percent of small business owners who were struggling or failing said not being organized affected their companies' productivity levels.[16]

"All generalizations are false. Including this one."

Mark Twain, American author and humorist

I've always compared using a business operating system to running a franchise. Having owned numerous franchises, I know the common denominator that brings you closer to success is following *their* system of success. A foundational operating system brings a company closer to franchising—having consistent, reproduceable results, and eliminates unknown and unpleasant surprises.

While the reported failure rates of franchises versus independent businesses are wildly inconsistent, according to a Forbes.com article, the rate of business failure is generally lower with franchises than with independent startups.[17] In addition, according to Seedcamp, a business that has its act together—is in a hot sector, has a functioning product, has traction, and has a strong management team—will garner more interest, and more dollars, from investors than one that's struggling in those areas.[18]

There are a few business operating systems available out there, including the Great Game of Business, Scaling Up, and EOS. Personally, I chose EOS because it worked for me; I was attracted to it because of its simplicity and the accelerated results I experienced. For example, I was able to take a marginally profitable wholesaling/distribution company with fewer than 1,000 customers to more than 8,000 by successfully implementing EOS, really *franchising* that business. It is that effective.

"I love deadlines. I like the whooshing sound they make as they fly by."
Douglas Adams, English author and screenwriter

When it comes to implementing a business operating system in a company the rules are simple, use only one, be fully committed to the journey of implementation, and as a leader, you must want to change for the better.

The Role Of Process

I want to talk about process for a minute. Development of your critical, core processes is significantly important to scaling your business. EOS has an interesting tool that focuses on the 20 percent of processes that will result in achieving 80 percent of your organizational success. I agree with that concept, however, I have also found that documenting your core processes using "Lean Thinking" will supercharge scalable growth. In the end you will build something that will lead employees in knowing what their roles are and create extreme clarity of what success looks like. Not creating a knee high SOP that nobody reads or understands. In the case of process—simpler is always better, regardless of the size of business.

According to research conducted by my company, only one in eight businesses have anything remotely considered to be an effective standard operating procedure.

Too much knowledge is kept in people's heads; there is no thought of using a keep-it-simple perspective and documenting those processes. What if someone who's critical to the company gets hit by a bus, is sick, quits, whatever the case may be? In most cases, there are no processes in place to support a *next-person-up* concept. We see this repeatedly, and I get why it happens. People are running their company. I fell into the trap, too; we were busy doing our jobs.

The issue, however, is if you lack process development, you can't leverage consistency and scalability. And at the end of the day, that is a major, major problem. When processes are defined, you don't have to worry about the next person up or having to judge performance against the process. It just makes for a better scenario and is part of putting your business in a box or franchising it.

BULLET DODGERS

Define Your Scalable Growth Architecture

Focus on the four building blocks in any order:

1. **Prioritized Leadership**—Never forget that success starts at the top. You must develop your own leadership skills and make sure you have a strong leadership team in place to support you.

2. **The Right People and Resources**—It's certainly worth the effort it takes to determine people's true probability of success before hiring them, and remember, all your resources won't be in-house.

3. **Dynamic Roadmap**—Ensure it's an absolute necessity to have access to good, hard, reliable data.

4. **Strong Operating Foundation**—Focus on strengthening the six key components of the business as well as "Leaning Out" your critical, core processes.

PART III

What's Next: Sustaining Scalable Growth

As you know, there is no finish line when you're running a business, no magical accomplishment that results in being able to say, "I'm done. I did it." This is especially true if you are an entrepreneur who strives to constantly take your business to the next level. Even after you have your SGA in place, you can't relax and enjoy the moment; you need to be continually addressing each of the four building blocks—prioritized leadership, the right people and resources, a strong operational foundation, and a dynamic roadmap—to ensure you're able to sustain scalable growth.

Like I mentioned before, this is not going to be doable for all business owners. But I'm thinking that since you're still reading, you're an entrepreneur who's not satisfied with the status quo, understands where you want to go, and is willing to put in the hard work necessary to build and sustain a scalable business—one that can overcome adversity in the long term.

CHAPTER 5

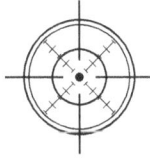

Create A Bulletproof Culture

"If you wait long enough, difficult people either quit, retire or die. That's my management style."

Before I wrap things up, let me share a few words about the role culture plays in ensuring your business is bulletproof. As I said previously, success will always start at the top, and one of the best things you can do as a leader is ensure you have a strong organizational culture that binds employees together for a common purpose.

Organizational culture has never been more important for small and midsized businesses, because of these seven reasons:[19]

- It defines your company's internal and external identity

- It's about living your company's core values

- It can transform employees into advocates (or critics)

- It helps you keep your best people

- It assists with onboarding

- It transforms your company into a team

- It impacts performance and employee well-being

When you hire people who exhibit your core values—people who can think like owners and have a vested interest in the success of the company—you enhance your culture on an ongoing basis, making it more robust and a significant differentiator as you work to maintain scalable growth.

Also important is keeping your finger on the pulse of the company—being proactive in seeking feedback that can inform your decision-making. Learning what's on the minds of customers, suppliers, and other stakeholders on a regular basis is key, as well as understanding what your employees are thinking.

I worked with an accounting firm that instituted daily huddles to secure feedback from employees on topics like what they could do better and if everyone was on board regarding its culture. This is an excellent way to ensure that no culture-sapping feelings seep into your team and negatively affect your business.

BULLET DODGERS

Create A Bulletproof Culture

1. Remember there is no finish line in business.

2. Build a business culture that reflects your values and binds your team together for a common purpose.

3. Never forget the importance of getting internal and external feedback on a regular basis.

CHAPTER 6

Say Goodbye To Mediocrity

GLASBERGEN ©Glasbergen

"There is always room for improvement. It's a
small room with no windows or distractions.
We already moved your things."

So here we are at the end. I've thrown quite a bit at you, but I hope you're energized about what is possible.

What differentiates the businesses that fail from those that succeed? In a nutshell, the latter are nimble enough to react, adapt, and overcome any threat—and thus have the ability to survive and thrive when all hell is breaking loose. Their owners have prepared their businesses to withstand anything that comes their way: They have bulletproofed their businesses.

The fact is, when you prepare your business for scalability and growth, in essence, you are also preparing it to deal with unforeseen curveballs.

The foundation or platform that is created when you want to take your business to the next level will also protect it when weathering any storm. It is an absolute differentiator and the reason why some businesses last while many fall by the wayside.

APPENDIX

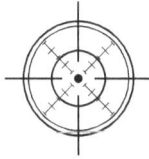

Acknowledgments

When I was asked to list acknowledgments for this book, I thought about my life's journey, my family, and people I have met who helped me see the light and understand there are no boundaries to success and there can be no regrets in life.

So here it goes. Thank you to:

- My mom, who taught me to be an entrepreneur before I even knew what one was

- My wife, who guided me with common sense and logic, because if she didn't,

I would have been bankrupt numerous times over

- My kids, for putting up with a workaholic entrepreneurial dad

- Sam Cupp, who trusted me as a friend, mentor, and business partner

- Everyone I come in contact with every day, because learning and growing never ends

About The Author

Rick Cottrell is the CEO of BizResults.com, a company that helps small-to-midsized companies bulletproof their businesses to survive and thrive in any economy. He has over thirty-five years of entrepreneurial business ownership experience—with fourteen cross-industry businesses and counting—has been awarded the SBA Small Business Advocate of the Year and was voted the Top Business Growth Advisor in St. Louis.

Rick is also a Certified EOS Implementer and has designed several proprietary products that focus on helping small-to-midsized businesses achieve predictable, scalable growth. He was the original developer of Salesforce.com and pioneered research in the CRM industry by developing solutions to support intelligent customer engagement and satisfaction strategies.

Rick has spoken to tens of thousands of people around the globe. He enjoys speaking on topics including business acceleration, sales and marketing innovation, and the future of the customer experience—and his energy, passion, and business knowledge ensure attendees walk away from his sessions with clarity, focus, and useful takeaways that can help them become more profitable in their businesses.

Considered a subject matter expert, Rick has been highlighted in many publications including the *Wall Street Journal*, *Harvard Business Review*, and *CEO Magazine* for his work with predictive business analytics and key performance metrics.

People do business with Rick Cottrell and BizResults. com for one simple reason—Rick has been there and done that. He is one of the most sought-after business growth advisors, having developed a proven set of systems, tools, and disciplines guaranteed to help any small-to-midsized business in any industry predictably scale and grow.

Learn more at https://bizresults.com or contact Rick directly at info@bizresults.com.

ENDNOTES

1   Remember the 1993 fantasy comedy film *Groundhog Day* starring Bill Murray as a cynical TV weatherman who finds himself reliving the same day over and over again?

2   "Study: 40 Percent of Businesses Fail to Reopen after a Disaster," Access, April 21, 2020, https://www.accesscorp.com/access-in-the-news/study-40-percent-businesses-fail-reopen-disaster/.

3   Ibid.

4   Brian Moran, "I Lost My Small Business in the Great Recession, but at Least I Learned How to Prepare for the Next One," CNBC, October 21, 2019, https://www.cnbc.com/2019/10/20/i-lost-my-business-in-great-recession-im-prepared-for-next-one.html.

5   James C. Collins, *Good to Great* (London: Random House Business, 2001).

6   Stephanie Burns, "7 Reasons to Join a Mastermind Group", *Forbes*, https://www.forbes.com/sites/chicceo/2013/10/21/7-reasons-to-join-a-mastermind-group.

7   "Nearly Three in Four Employers Affected by a Bad Hire, According to a Recent CareerBuilder Survey," CareerBuilder website press release, December 7, 2017, http://press.careerbuilder.com/2017-12-07-Nearly-Three-in-Four-Employers-Affected-by-a-Bad-Hire-According-to-a-Recent-CareerBuilder-Survey.

8.   "Why New Hires Fail (Emotional Intelligence Vs. Skills)," Leadership IQ (blog), accessed April 16, 2020, https://www.leadershipiq.com/blogs/leadershipiq/35354241-why-new-hires-fail-emotional-intelligence-vs-skills.

9. Lisa Frye, "The Cost of a Bad Hire Can Be Astronomical," SHRM, August 16, 2019, https://www.shrm.org/resourcesand-tools/hr-topics/employee-relations/pages/cost-of-bad-hires.aspx.

10. Arlene S. Hirsch, "Don't Underestimate the Importance of Good Onboarding," SHRM, August 10, 2017, https://www.shrm.org/resourcesandtools/hr-topics/talent-acquisition/pages/dont-underestimate-the-importance-of-effective-onboarding.aspx.

11. "Making the Case for Professional Development Benefits," SHRM, January 30, 2018, https://www.shrm.org/hr-today/trends-and-forecasting/research-and-surveys/pages/2017-employee-benefits-professional-development.aspx.

12. Arlene S. Hirsch, "Don't Underestimate the Importance of Good Onboarding," SHRM, August 10, 2017, https://www.shrm.org/resourcesandtools/hr-topics/talent-acquisition/pages/dont-underestimate-the-importance-of-effective-onboarding.aspx.

13. Ibid.

14. Dan Sullivan, *The Dan Sullivan Question*, (Toronto: The Strategic Coach, Inc., 2009).

15. Gino Wickman. *Traction: Get a Grip on Your Business*. (Dallas: BenBella Books, 2012).

16. Michael Guta, "75% Of Struggling Small Business Owners Believe Being Disorganized Leads to Productivity Loss," *Small Business Trends*, February 7, 2018, https://smallbiztrends.com/2018/02/being-disorganized-leads-to-productivity-loss.html.

17. Fiona Simpson, "To Buy Or Not To Buy—Taking On A Franchise Versus Going It Alone," Forbes.com, September 25, 2018, https://www.forbes.com/sites/fionasimpson1/2018/09/25/to-buy-or-not-to-buy-taking-on-a-franchise-versus-going-it-alone/#1773e1e2859d.

18. Carlos Eduardo Espinal, "How Does an Early-Stage Investor Value a Startup?" Seedcamp, accessed April 23, 2020, https://seedcamp.com/resources/how-does-an-early-stage-investor-value-a-startup.

19. Corey Moseley, "7 Reasons Why Organizational Culture Is Important," Jostle.com (blog), accessed June 18, 2020, https://blog.jostle.me/blog/why-is-organizational-culture-important.